PSALMS OF LIFE

A BOOK OF POETRY

BY

CAROLYN STOVALL

ISBN: Jasmaya Productions and Publications 978-0-9966565-8-0 10000 E.Paseo San Ardo Tucson, Arizona, 85747

JASMAYA
Productions & Publications
The Eyes of Independent Publishing

Foreword

I was given the honor to write few words concerning the author of this great work of encouragement and inspiration, Carolyn Stovall. I have known Carolyn Stovall since I was a child. She just happens to be my big sister. I affectionately call her Caddy (after the book "Caddy Woodlawn"). She became one of my heroes after I realized the great service and sacrifice she has shared with God's people when I was in my middle to late twenties (many years ago).

Carolyn Stovall (Caddy) is one of the most caring and loving individuals you would ever want to meet. She exemplifies the "Christian" virtue of hospitality. She has given of herself and her resources, with the blessing of her husband Ted most of the time, untiringly. I have known of her taking home strangers from an airport she met on the plane who had no ride and/or nowhere to stay. She has fed countless numbers of people, including armed services personnel and their families, many more times than I can count. Caddy meets no strangers. To her they are all God's children and are to be treated as such.

Carolyn Stovall has served as the adult Sunday school teacher at Lackland Air force Base for over 20 years. She is the kind of teacher who encourages her students to become the teacher. She received a Masters in Community Counseling and used that training as a family counselor with Baptist Child and Family Services (BCFS) until she retired. Carolyn would sometimes encourage her clients with some of her poetry. Carolyn shares her poetry wherever God gives her the opportunity.

I believe that you will find something in these pages of poetry that will encourage, inspire and put a smile on your face. That is what Carolyn Stovall's poetry does for me and with others whom she has shared her poetry. Enjoy!

Rita Kittrell
Sister in Christ and in the flesh.

A Note From The Author's Mother

Carolyn is the eldest of my four daughters who God has given a talent to recite and write Christian poetry. The Bible tells us not to hide our talents under a bushel basket, and Carolyn certainly has not done that. She feels this is God's gift to share.

In 1983, I remember going to a Sunday Service at P.T. L. (Praise The Lord). After the service I was looking for Carolyn and she was standing at the front entrance giving out pamphlets of her poetry.

All through the years people have been enjoying her poetry. If anyone asks for a copy of one of her poems she would take their e-mail address and send it to then because she wanted then to enjoy her poems. She believes that God has meant for them to be shared. I am delighted that God has opened this opportunity to have her poems published. Her poems are inspirational and spiritual.

Bettye Lewis

ACKNOWLEDGEMENTS

God is truly the head of my life. It has been many years ago that the Lord so graciously gave me the gift of Poetry. Truthfully it was not a gift I wanted. I have shared the gift with people all over the world.

I want to sincerely thank my husband Ted H. Stovall for his love and patience.
Also, I would like to thank my family and friends for their loyal support, and encouraging words. Finally I'd like to thank my publisher, my cousin Kambon Obayani/Jasmaya Production and Publications.

MAY I PRAY WITH YOU?

I'm sorry that you are not feeling
Very well today
But Jesus told me to call on you
To encourage you on your way
My name is Carolyn Stovall
And Jesus is my friend
He blessed me with his Spirit
And now Jesus lives within
I'm striving to be like Jesus
More and more each day
I've come to help brighten up your day
Do you mind if we might pray

Table of Contents

Psalms of Life
Anguish/Pain

ALL ALONE

I said I would be your servant
Lord, I promise to obey
But it seems as if I sometimes feel
That I have strayed away

I feel as if I'm all alone
With no one to really care
And heavy with my burdens, Lord
No one with whom to share

I feel like I want to cry
Perhaps to release the pain
But without a touch from you Master
The burdens remain the same

BROKEN HEARTED

I know your heart is broken

And tears they just won't cease

Your thoughts they just keep racing

It feels like there is no relief

You hate to recall the story

For it grieves your heart inside

Withdrawal and isolation

Because peace does not abide

There is a God of comfort

And He knows the pain you bear

He'll strengthen you in your darkest hour

Go to Him, He will always be there

CLOSER TO THEE

Lord, I need to get closer, closer to thee

Lord, I need to get closer, won't you humble me please

Lord, I need to get closer, I can't stand it where I am

Father, hear me, hear me, won't you please give me
your hand

Lord, I need to get closer, loose the bonds of chains I
am in

Lord, I need to get closer, please cleanse my heart of
sin

Lord, I am tired of these shackles weighing me down

There's no love, there's no joy, no peace can be found

Lord, I need to get closer, closer to thee

Lord, I need to get closer, closer to thee

Take me as I am, won't you draw me near

Keep my feet from falling, wash away all my fears

And let me seek your face until my time has come

Let your grace sustain me, Lord, let your will be done

CONSTANT COMPLAINING

Perhaps this may be offensive
But these words I have to say
Constantly complaining of life's trials
Are pushing people away

We all have some problems
And some are heavy to bear
But when you continuously dwell on them
It is a pity party you want us to share

So I hope that in the future
As the years fly by
Perhaps you'll look for something good in the bad
And there be joy for the tears you cried

CONTINUANCE

So heavy is my heart Lord,
The load is hard to bear
The tears roll down my face
It's because of you Lord that I care

I want to love my neighbor
And love those who do wrong to me
I'll continue to bear the cross Lord
To be clothed in humility

I'll continue to spread your word, Lord
Even when I feel so small
Surrendering my life to you Jesus
Just to answer Lord your call

I'll continue to love my neighbor
No matter who it is or where ever I may be
I promise to continue to follow you Lord,
That my life will be pleasing to thee

DELIVER US

Deliver us O Lord we pray
From all the fear that comes our way
Fear of failure
Fear to achieve
Fear to be obedient
Fearful to receive
Fear of being rejected
Fear of being alone
Fear of trusting you Father
Fearful of the unknown
Deliver us O lord we pray
We refuse to be defeated
By fear another day

DRINK OF THE CUP

Suffering and sorrow go hand and hand
But it takes us awhile to understand
Drink of the cup the Lord gives to each one
For His perfect will must be done
No matter what it is you must go on through
For joy and peace is waiting for you

EXISTING

Do you call it living or existing
In a world where no one cares
And you try so very hard
But, you're overtaken with despair

You can't seem to find the happiness
In the things that you can buy
Not even with your education
But you try and try and try

Success it seems the ultimate
So you work hard everyday
Struggling, and struggling to make it
But the peace never seems to stay

FEELINGS

Father, I lay my feelings upon the alter

In the quietness in my little heart

At any given minute Lord

The tears might right now start

I am really having a struggle Lord

But I know what I must do

I guess I carried it far too long

Here at the alter I give it to you

I know the Holy Spirit

Will give me the peace I need

Comfort my little heart dear Lord

Forgive this anxiety

GIVE ME PEACE

All doubt and fears are surfacing
Lord, what is it that I must do?
Please give me new revelation
As I try to pray my way through

I know I am not to worry
Anxiety is a sin
Lord I am trying my best to be patient
I seem to be overwhelmed within

I'm crying Abba Father
Lord set my mind at ease
Please come thou Holy Spirit come
And give me the peace I need

GOD HAS A PLAN

It's sad to see you suffering

And makes us want to cry

We've asked the Lord continuously

Lord, why, oh why, oh why

But God he has a plan for you

Though we don't understand

Yes, tears and joy and suffering

Are apart of God's own plan

He will turn your midnight into joy

Yes, sadness will slowly fade

He'll renew your hope in Him again

His love He'll not take away

GOD KNOWS THE BURDEN

For in the time of trouble

Despair and so much grief

Seek God and He will carry you

And give your soul relief

God knows the burden that you bear

How you feel you can't go on

He will uphold you with His hand

And shelter you from this storm

He'll be your strength when you are weak

He'll build new hope again

Child, even in this trial you must trust Him

He's your God, your Saviour, and your friend

HURT AND HEARTACHE

There is a hurt that you will bear
Only because you really care
Remember the Lord will take you through
Even though there are times you don't want Him to

The heartache will come
And despair you will know
But patience and love will begin to show
Pick up the cross continue to go

The journey is tedious and sometimes slow
Surrender your will let the Lord direct the way
And when you fall down
Child, remember to pray

LONGING

I've longed for someone to love me

And to accept me

And I've failed to find it

In friends, work or family

I've prayed and hoped

That there was someone

Who would care?

I heard the Lord say

My child, my child it's not there

Come unto me I accept you

You are mine

All that I have child, I will give

But it is going to take some time

MY GRACE IS SUFFICIENT FOR THEE

When you are all alone

And in despair

Given up on life

To where you just don't care

My grace is sufficient for thee

When you have no money

To buy new shoes

Your clothes wearing thin

And not enough food

My grace is sufficient for thee

Running from your problems

Here and there

Can't find any peace

Not anywhere

My grace is sufficient for thee

Even if you are sick or a cripple

Or you are laid up in bed

The pain is so great

You would rather die instead

My Grace is sufficient for thee

The grace that I speak of

Is from God above

Who is constantly showering us

With His grace and perfect love

My grace is sufficient for thee

REJECTION

The God of this world hath blinded their minds

And Lord they cannot see

For Lord they cannot understand

That they are hurting me

Overwhelmed by rejection

Humiliated by their fear

Scorned and shunned and dramatized

My heart cries many tears

But Father will you forgive them

For they know not what they do

As I recall the scripture

Jesus suffered the same way too

SO MANY TIMES

So many times
When I feel so strong
Everything I do
It seems to come out wrong

So many times
When I lose my way
So many times
I forget to pray

So many times
My mind seems confused
Frustrated and depressed
All I hear is bad news

So many times
When I fall apart
Dear heavenly Father
Please search my heart

STANDING IN NEED

I'm searching heavenly Father
I'm searching yes indeed
O Father won't you help me
For I'm standing here in need

My mind is twisted and confused
I don't know what to do
I've tried to solve it on my own
But, I can't so I'm asking you

I cannot eat or cannot sleep
My heart is swelled within
This is a heavy load for me
And I know that this is sin

I want to serve you Lord,
And I want to do what's right
But my mind and thoughts are hassled
From sunrise till the sun sets at night

Please help me heavenly Father
Do what you think is best
And cleanse my filthy heart, Lord
And set my soul at rest

SUFFERING

Lord, Let us drink of the bitter cup

As we walk the narrow way

Let us share in your suffering

That you may be glorified in us today

Let us visualize the cross

The excruciating pain you had to bear

Let us remember how much you loved us

All alone you hung up there.

SUFFERING AND SORROW

Suffering and sorrow

Seem to never end

But please be patient

And wait my friend

Joy is sorrow that is overcome

For this is when the transforming is done

When nights of sorrow visit your way

Don't fear or dread them

They are not here to stay

THINKING

I always seem to be thinking,
Thinking, thinking
Of things I have to do
The more I seem to dwell on them
The more I get confused

The more I get confused
The more I get depressed
And then my little soul
Can find no peace or rest

The more I get frustrated
The bigger the problem seems to be
And then I completely forget
To turn it over to thee

TOO MUCH TO BEAR

Was it too much suffering?
You find it too much to bear
Did you feel all alone?
Or wrecked with despair

Perhaps there was no teaching
And you didn't know what to do
You tried hard to live holy
And how to pray your way through

Perhaps you couldn't see
The Lord's will for your life
You allowed Satan to creep in
Bringing confusion and strife
The fruit of the spirit
I know you just couldn't see

The Lord is building His character
Through patience and humility
Longsuffering is a fruit
Just as well as joy and peace
Meekness, gentleness, temperance
Remember His love will not cease

Let the flesh be crucified
With the affections and lust inside
Let Him renew you in the spirit
Let His perfect peace abide

WHY?

Why do I feel so weepy?
Tears swelling up in my eyes
Why is my heart just aching?
And the emptiness inside

Why is this life so lonely?
Why am I to go alone?
Why do I just keep roaming?
No place to call my home

Is this the way you traveled Lord
Could you have felt this way
Did the tears roll down your face Lord
As the people turned away

Psalms of Life
Children

THE CHALLENGING CHILD

As I fight against that dominating spirit
That says I must have my own way
To make my own decisions
For I have plotted my course for today

Everyday there is a battle
For you to do just as you please
Challenging my authority
But let me put you're mind at ease

You've been entrusted to me for a period of time
I must train you in the way to go
To love, to help, to direct your path
I understand that you need room to grow

There are things that I will require of you
And there are rules that you must obey
I know that you will challenge me
But guess who lost again today?

THE CHILDREN ARE WATCHING

Did you know the children are watching?
Every move that you make
Did you know the children are watching?
Trying to figure out what road to take
Did you know the children are watching?

The blemishes in your life
And they will follow in your footsteps
They will pick up jealousy, hatred, envy and strife
Did you know the children are watching?

How is your life today?
Is the love of Jesus in focus?
In any kind of way
Did you stop just long enough?
To give thanks to God or even pray
Did you know the children are watching?

How about a new example today
Accept Jesus as your personal Saviour
And let Jesus show you the right way
Did you know the children are watching?

TRAIN THEM

Children have no direction
When they are born into this life
They have no real conception
Of the things that are wrong or right

And this is why the lord
Has placed them in your hands
To try to teach his children
Try to make them understand

For children can only see
What's best for them today
But you as parents can see
A little farther down the way

People please wake up
For the time is now at hand
For what you teach your children
They will carry
When they become a woman or a man

YOU WERE CHOSEN BY THE FATHER

Before the foundations of the earth
You were chosen by the Father above
To become a part of our family
To experience God's genuine love

God designed the way He wants you to be
You've been fashioned by the Master's hand
And set you on a course that you experience each day
As you learn the things that God has planned

We will share and love and guide your path
In the way God expects you to go
We want you to know that we love you
And will encourage and will help you to grow

We want you to know that we love you
Even though you may not always understand
We may make some mistakes along life roads
But remember God's original plan

Trials and tribulations of life will come
Our love and support will be there
We are committed to nurture, to help and to guide
To show you that we really care…

Psalms of Life
DEATH/DYING

AN APPOINTED TIME

Everyday someone is dying
Some are young and some are old
Some we are surprised at
And some we wish they would hurry up and go

Some are very fearful
And they fight hard to remain here
They try out every solution to stay
For their life is very dear

Some are relieved and willing
For they know Christ as Saviour and Lord
And He will usher them into His kingdom
And their blessings will be restored

Some are peaceful even in suffering
They're not grumpy not at all
But resting in God's promises
And listening for His call

So matter where you are in life
It doesn't matter if you are rich or poor
There is an appointed time for us all
He will one day knock on your hearts door

ARE YOU READY

The time is drawing nigh
The Saviours' soon to come
For He is coming to redeem
The faithful holy ones

Are you ready, are you ready
This may be your last day
When you stand before the judgment seat
Have you thought of words to say

Have you tried to live in the world?
Did you compromise at all?
Did you extend a helping hand?
When someone was about to fall?

Did you give some extra food?
Maybe some clothes to wear
Did you try to let your neighbor know?
Behind the walls you really did care

Did you try to live in peace?
And to walk in harmony
Or was it only doing
What was the very best for" me"

We're going to all have to come together
For it's going to be that way up there
Unless we come together here
I don't think we will be going anywhere

IN THE BATTLE

I called you to be a soldier
So come to battle with me
I promise to lead and guide you
And never stray from thee

There'll be some wounded on the road
And some will even die
Pick up the cross and follow me
For Zion is in sight

Accept the roads I've prepared for you
For I know the way to go
Often times the journey will seem
Like the pace is very slow

Just trust in Me
Just trust in me
I can see what lies ahead
With the things I give to equip you
Your soul shall always be fed

You may lose this mortal body
Since it is doomed to die
But there will be no more tears
Or no more pain
For the end is eternal life

NUMBERED DAYS

Death we do not understand
There's despair and so much grief
We ask the question why O Lord
The pain finds no relief

Our days are numbered by the Lord
We don't know when, where, or how
We must be ready when He call for us
It could be this very hour

He will give you peace in the midst of the storm
You must seek Him every day
As you surrender your will to Jesus
He'll instill hope along life's way

The bond of love will not be broken
Cherished memories will never fade
Our God has not abandoned you
He will carry you through these hard days

REMEMBER

If you don't see me on tomorrow
And I have gone to be at rest
Just hold on tight to Jesus and you follow
And try to do your very best

The tears that roll down on your face
And grief and burdens that you bear
Cast them to Jesus and with haste
Because Jesus really cares

I've gone home to be with Jesus
Please don't cry no more for me
Comfort the others when it's needed
And ask them to always remember me

Remember the love of Jesus I always tried to share
And you follow the footsteps of Jesus
So you can walk in heaven
One day with Jesus and me there...

WASHED IN THE BLOOD OF THE LAMB

Only those who's been washed

In the blood of the Lamb

Who is pure and clean inside

Only those who've confessed Christ

As Saviour and Lord in His presence shall abide

Only those who flee from lustful acts

And do that which is right

Only those who seek those heavenly things

Shall see God's holy light

Who shall abide, Lord who shall abide

Lord teach me the perfect way

I want to see you face to face

When you come for me that day

WE DO NOT UNDERSTAND

Death we do not understand
Despair and so much grief
We ask the question why O Lord
The pain finds know relief

Our days are numbered by the Lord
We don't know when, where or how
We must be ready when He calls for us
It could be this very hour

He will give you peace in the midst of the storm
You must seek Him everyday
As you surrender your will to Jesus
He'll instill peace along life's way

The bond of love will not be broken
Cherished memories will never fade
Our God has not abandoned you
He will carry you through these hard days

WHAT WILL THEY SAY ABOUT YOU?

What will they say about you?
When your time has slipped away
What will God say about you?
When you meet the Saviour that day

Will He say "thou good and faithful servant"
Your reward is in my hand
You have a home in glory
In that far and distant land

I've seen your trials and tribulations
All the suffering you've been through
This brand new home in glory
Has been reserved in heaven just for you

Your work on earth's complete
And now your time is passed
You now have a glorified body
That's finally free at last

Psalms of Life
EMPOWER/service

A DIFFERENT PATH

As I traveled through life's journey
There were choices that I made
That took me far from Jesus
And my spiritual life did fade

I hid those things which no one knew
Yes, the streets did call my name
Even tried to take my life one day
Because I lived in sin and shame

Then one day so unexpectedly
There was a knock at my front door
She said that Jesus loved me
Yes, I've heard that message before

I questioned, "How could Jesus love me?"
Someone as bad as me
Can He forgive the things I've done
And set my spirit free

He'll cleanse, restore, and give you hope
Yes, He'll place His spirit inside
And He'll lead you down a different path
For His spirit will be your guide

It's all because of His great love
And the cross of Calvary
He hung and died and rose again
For you unconditionally

A SEARCH FOR FREEDOM

Lord, I need to be free

From the sinful things

That's surrounding me

Not so much of material things

But what my selfish nature brings

There's so much Lord

Of things here for me

But I want the things

You've prepared for me

I want to be whole

Not pieces and parts

I want your love within my heart

I want to do good things for you

That you may be glorified

In the thing that I do

AN INSTRUMENT

During my life Lord
Please use me to make a difference
In the world to all mankind
Give me heavenly visions
Being creative in my mind
Using gift, and talents
Surrendering my will to you
Being a living vessel
Just someone you might use

Use me to make a difference
Showing someone that I really care
I'll even go the extra mile
And try my best to share
Please use me to spread your vision
That salvation you freely give
Lord let me be an example
And share your love
That we might live

ANYWHERE

Perhaps you may be behind a prison wall
But God can use you anywhere
Try responding to his call

You may have had your share
Of suffering and pain
Try trusting in the Saviour
For you've really much to gain

And tears you may have cried
Till it seems like there's no more
But joy will come into your heart
And peace unknown before

Yes, God can use you anywhere
And there's so much He wants you to do
But you have to surrender your will to Him
For God to work a miracle through you

BECAUSE THAT'S JUST WHO I AM

I gave my heart to you
To help in any way that I can
To serve with a willing heart
To every child, woman, boy or man

I knew it would be a sacrifice
For Jesus did this just for me
He shed His blood He hung and died
On the cross of Calvary

He bore the pain upon that cross
While others mocked him so
He never mumbled not even a word
They tried to humiliate him so

He told the thief upon the cross
You will be in heaven now with me
I died and rose again my friend
And now you can be free

Do the work that I have called you to do
Don't worry what men may say
For we will all have to give an account
When we meet God on judgment day

CHANGE THOU ME

Change thou me O Lord
Change thou me
For I am crying out for help
Down here on my knees

I give it all up Lord
Help me will you please
Make me whole, make me new
Make me fitting unto thee

My thoughts are not pure
And evil lies in my heart
Cleanse thou me O Lord,
So I can have a new start

Selfishness is not
Any of your ways
Replace it with love
In my heart today

Change thou me O Lord,
Change thou me
So I can be an example
So that others just might see

The new life
The new change
That Jesus has given me
Dear Lord, Change thou me

EXAMINE ME

Examine me O Lord and see

If there be any sin

Unclean thing deep inside of me

Then wash it away

Make me whiter than snow

Dear Jesus I want you to be

In complete control

Then try me Lord, so that I might stand

Will you lead and guide me upon this land

And if I stumble and fall along the way

Will you pick me up and show me the right way

For I truly want to see you face to face

One blessed holy day

FOOTSTEPS OF JESUS

I want to walk in your footsteps
Follow in your ways
Spread the love you've given me
To others everyday

I want to be filled by your spirit
Till my cup overflows
I want to be constantly lead and guided
For you to be in control

I want to be hungry for your word
For it to fill my heart within
I want to be free from evil thoughts
And my soul completely cleansed

I want the light of Jesus to shine
So that others will be able to see
I want to abide in you Christ Jesus
And for you to abide in me

FRESH ANOINTING

I need a fresh anointing
I need another touch
I need your power in my life
I need it oh so much

I believe that you are powerful
Mighty, holy, and strong
I need you heavenly Father
Draw me now where I belong

I see so much around me
I don't know what to do
If you will now refill me
So that I may glorify you

I need a fresh anointing
Send your power now I pray
I want to surrender my will to you Lord
So you can be glorified in my life today

GIVING A HELPING HAND

There are some jobs we feel
That are beneath us and we won't do
But it's through the lowly stuff
Where God's blessing comes flowing through

It's when we give a helping hand
And walk the extra mile
We can really feel good about one self
And put on an honest smile

It's when we try our best
To do all that we can do
Treating your neighbor as thyself
It God's commandment He gives to you

GOD IS NOT PLEASED

Fix our own blessing

Pave our own way

Condemn people in their thinking

Pressuring them to what we feel and say

Then when they have surrendered

We say look what God has done

Just look how he has blessed us

I know I'm the chosen one

But God is not pleased

He'll expose the hidden sin

It was not His blessings not at all

It was your selfishness my friend.

HOPELESS

I feel like it's a hopeless situation

And I like to run away

Lord, I don't want to deal with

Perhaps on some other day

Lord I know that it will be painful

As you reveal evil in my heart

Maybe you can do it a little at a time

Lord, today do you have to start?

Lord I know I shouldn't go on feelings

For they tend to always deceive

For we walk by faith and not by sight

Or how it feels to me

So Lord I'll let you have these feelings

And Lord please have your perfect way

Just shape me, make me

The way you want me to be

Lord, please don't wait another day

I AM WILLING

Lord, my voice I sometimes quiver
And my vocabulary isn't too great
My clothes are kind of outdated
And amongst crowds I tend to shake

But nevertheless I'm willing
To speak the word that you give
Whether the task is great or small
I promise to obey as long as I live

But nevertheless I'm willing to speak
The words that you give
Whether the task is great or small
I promise to obey as long as I live

I know my anxiety, tears, and fears
You can wipe away
So father, I humbly bow before you
Let me glorify you today

I WILL NOT COMPROMISE

They say I must accept it

I say that I cannot

They say that I must compromise

I say that I cannot be bought

They say it must be overlooked

Don't let it get you down

I say I cannot close my eyes

Lord I cannot be bound

They say it's been for many years

It's time to change I say

You cannot live in yester-year

You must live for today

IMITATION

Imitate me wherever you go
Let the love of Jesus always show
Charity suffers long
And is kind to one another
It is not puffed up
Nor envies his brother

It is not unmannerly or conceited
And seeks not his own
Nor does it take account of wrong
And sits and groans and moans

It is not easily provoked
Or thinks in evil ways
Rejoices not in iniquity
But truth from day to day

It bears everything in silence
And has unquenchable faith
It hopes in all kinds of circumstances
Endurance never lost a race

His love will never fail you
No matter where you go
Just ask the heavenly Father
To let His begin to show

INNOCENCE

I sought to prove my innocence
Of charges made against me
Revenge and bitterness did infest
Instead of humility

I tried so hard to forgive
To replace the pain with love
A continuous surrender of my will
And seeking His will above

I am seeking you heavenly Father
Please help me to overcome
The trials and tribulations
Gaining victory over every one

Not for me to boast Lord
For the glory all is thine
But for me to be obedient
And for thy will to be mine

LACKING IN PRAYER

When I think about our relationship Lord,
I can plainly see
That I have been lacking in my prayer life
I've failed to talk to thee

In my heart I know I should take the time
But the moment quickly slips away
I tend to fill my mind with things and concerns
That I thought I needed that day

I contemplate, I reason
Never once have I thought of you
Sometimes I'll offer up a real small prayer
I don't believe that you will come through

I know that you are drawing me
To this quiet place of Prayer
To listen, and wait expectedly
Knowing you will meet me there

So I ask you to forgive me
Change my heart so that I might pray
To learn to intercede for others
To make a difference in some small way

LAID UP

If I had to be laid up on a bed

And my only moveable parts

Were my hands and my head

My mouth could move

And my eyes could see

Could I except this as God's will for me?

Would I always complain?

Would I be hateful or unkind?

Would I dwell on self pity?

Or lose my mind?

Would I try to cheer someone else up everyday?

Surrendering to the Lord

To let Him have His own way

Only the Lord knows exactly what I would do

But I turn to you Father

For the grace to go on through

For no matter what it is

That you have prepared for me

I sincerely want to be obedient unto thee

MAKE ME SHAPE ME

Dear Jesus, wilt thou humble me
Make me, shape me, form me
The way you would have me to be
Examine me O Lord and see
If there be any sin, unclean thing
Deep inside of me
Please wash it away
Make me whiter than snow
Dear Jesus I want you to be in complete control
Then try me Lord, so that I might stand
Will you lead and guide me upon this land
And if I stumble and fall along the way
Please pick me up and show me the right way
For I truly want to see you face to face
One blessed holy day

PRIVATE PEOPLE

Private people here I find
Snobbish and cold hearted are their signs
When you need a helping hand
Oh they will do
But as soon as they are finished
Then are through with you

Behind the closed doors
They hover themselves
And they really don't care
About anyone else

One day before I met Jesus
I was kind of the same way
Keeping to myself
So I wouldn't be used day after day after day

But Jesus came in
And washed my fears and sins away
Filled me with His Holy Spirit
And now I am new
And I am not afraid
To do for you or you or you

Whatever it may be
To love, listen, help, pray, or share
I'm not a private people anymore
I really care

RUNNING THE RACE

Many will enter the race
Some are fast and some are slow
But those who endure to the end
Will win the prize you know

You must keep on running
Even though the way looks very dim
Looking to the Father
For the light shines only in Him

You must keep on running
Even though you are tired and very weak
Trusting in the Saviour's love
For Jesus promises you He will keep

Take another step
Keep on trusting day by day
He'll give you all the strength you need
To help you on your way

SOMEONE

My gift, Lord use it as you may

That I might comfort Someone along the way

Someone who is sick and stricken to a bed

To Someone who has a thirsty soul that needs to be fed

To Someone who is nice and is all alone

Or to Someone who isn't either

Or to Someone who doesn't have a home

To Someone who uses you

And find it hard to share

Or to Someone who has given up

And says I just don't care

To Someone who is hateful

To everyone around

Lord all of these Someones

In my life time I have found

So Lord I give you all these Someones

And put them in your care

And let this little Someone

Love, listen, help, pray or share

STEAL AWAY TO JESUS

Steal away to Jesus
Is what we need to do
An emptying of oneself
So the Spirit can teach you

Steal away to Jesus
And humbly bow in prayer
You can leave your cares with Jesus
His peace he'll give you there

Steal away to Jesus
In silence he knows best
By stealing away to Jesus
Your soul will find His rest

Come steal away to Jesus
As often as you can
By stealing away to Jesus
You can be refreshed, revived,
A renewed woman or man

WORLD OR GOD'S STANDARD

According to the world's standards
People view you as very bright
But talking about God's spiritual kingdom
You cannot shed any light

Do people see the Word of God?
As the main focus in your life
Or are you a messy person
Who stirs up jealousy, hatred, gossip and strife?

Do you hold on to offenses?
Remembering "all wrong things done to me"?
Or do you walk in forgiveness?
And setting others free

Do they see you trust the Saviour?
When there is no way out
Or do they see you always doubting
Entombed by fear, stress, anxiety and doubt?

We have a handbook for daily living
Peace and love Jesus constantly gives
You cannot let your mind be caught up
In worldly things by which we live

Psalms of Life
FAITH/PRAISE

A CHANGE, A CHANGE

A change a change has
come over me
Since the very
beginning
When Jesus set my soul
free
He began to cleanse my
heart within
Of all the filthy stains
of sin
I don't want to do the
things I did before
But just try to
understand me
They are no fun for me
anymore
The parties, the
drinking,
The staying out late and
getting high
Not really facing life
But letting it pass right
on by
And trying to keep up
with the fashions
And trying to stay real
cool
I want you to know
I was the biggest fool
Unhappy and unloved
But finding a little
comfort there
But hoping someone
Would understand me
and care
Then someone came
along
With a different love
you see

Not scheming, not
getting anything in
return
And not using me
Who told me about a
man
Who had died to set me
free
Who would give me
joy, in the midst of
sorrow
Peace, love, joy, life
abundantly
Accept Jesus as your
Saviour
And then you will see
Of all the wonderful
blessing
Jesus had in store for
me
Now this was a little
much
Real hard for me to
believe

But whatever Jesus
gave to me
I was more than willing
to receive
And this is the place
that I am at today
Jesus is continuously
changing my ways
To be more like Him
and less like me
Keeping me humble
So I can be of service,
to Him and to thee

BATTLE IS NOT YOURS

When the enemy comes to battle
He'll come with power and might
His job is to totally destroy you
And know, he will put up a good fight

He'll use intimidation
And persecute you in many ways
He'll try to make you fear him
And lead your heart astray

He will accuse you to the brethern
He'll rob your peace and rest
He'll make you doubt the Word of God
Remember this is only a test

You must set your heart to seek God
Stay on your knees in prayer
Ask the heavenly Father to help you
Stand fast for the Lord, He cares

Acknowledge you have no power or might
And you don't know what to do
But your eyes are fixed upon Jesus
For all power belongs to you

You need not to fight in this battle
Set yourself stand still and see
The salvation of the Lord your God
He's there to provide for thee

DON'T BE AFRAID

Don't be afraid, don't be afraid
For the Lord is there with you

Don't be afraid to trust him
So do the best that you can do

The gifts that God has given you
Don't tuck them neatly away

Glorify the Father right now
You're not promised another day

Don't be afraid, don't be ashamed
Faith will pave the way

Stretch out my child, Hold on to faith
Will you glorify the Lord today?

FAITH

Faith believes in God the Father
And in His beloved son

Faith is willing to take some risks in life
For the Father's will to be done

Faith it stands and does not wavier
No matter what the cost

Faith believes God's Word of promise
Though all physical gain is lost

Faith is sure that God is able
For He has the Master Plan

Faith believes God is creator
That your life is in His hand

Faith hopes that though I perish
That your spirit is alive

And you go down yet rejoicing
That our God be glorified

FAITH TO BELIEVE

I believe that they won't be tagged
For wrong things I've done before
Jesus forgave me of my sins
And he remembers my sin no more

So Satan you just get back
And leave my mind alone
There is no room for you here
Go find another home

I accepted the Word of God by faith
For He gave me faith to believe
I rebuke you in the name of Jesus
I command you now to flee

FATHER I NEED YOU

Lord, I don't see you, where are you?

You promised you would help me to go through

This journey seems so long and hard

Too much for me to bear

Father, you know that I need you

Please let me know that you are there

I need your hand to guide me

I need your light to shine

I need the calm assurance

To know for sure you're mine

GOD DOES NOT LIE

God does not lie
You must believe
Stand firm on His word
Only then will you receive

He's given you the Victory
But child you must go through
Stop striving against the spirit
Is there anything He cannot do

God is truth
Righteousness is His way
He'll lead you down the path he wants
You must trust Him child today

It doesn't matter about circumstance
Or what you can or cannot do
God does not lie you must believe
Cannot God work through you?

GRATEFUL

Jesus we are grateful for your love
For peace and joy that swells within
For cleansing us daily
From all of our sins

For faith and hope
That we can believe
And from you heavenly Father
Freely we can receive

For grace and mercy
That's has been multiplied
The confidence of knowing
Only on you we can rely

For shelter and food,
Yes peace and rest
We thank you Father
For you give us your best

HELPING ME GROW

Thank you heavenly Father for the suffering
Thank you for the pain
Thank you for the tears I cried
Over and over again

Thank you for the situation
How you allowed us to grow
Thank you for the Holy Spirit
Assuring me you were in control

Thank you for your love
That you gave me Lord each day
Thank you for your joyful showers
That showered me along the way

Thank you for the assurance
The victory's already won
By praying and waiting patiently for
Thy will on earth be done

HOW DO I KNOW YOU

How do I know you, Lord?
How do I know?
Just what you have in store for me
Or where am I to go
How can I seek your face?
How do I know that you are for real?
Is it written in the word of God?
That Jesus loves me still?

How can I accept you Lord?
There is no certificate for me
Is this what you meant by faith?
Trust you, you can't be seen
How can I hear your voice?
Can you really talk to me?
I'm searching heavenly Father
For my soul has a desperate need

And what's the Holy Spirit
That I hear people speaking of
Could this be the way?
That you send your precious love
How do I know you Lord?
How do I know?
No matter how long it takes for me
I promise not to let go

I'M NOT WORTHY

I'm not worthy of your blessings
No I'm not worthy not at all
I'm not worthy when my faith waivers
And I stumble along and fall

I'm not worthy when I grumble
About the trials that I go through
I'm not worthy when I drift
Farther and farther away from you

But, Thou alone art worthy,
A sacrifice made for me
For you bore my sin, and you set me free
On the cross of Calvary

How worthy art Thou O Lamb of God
And now I am worthy too
For without spot or blemish and perfect love
You redeemed mankind right back to you

IMPATIENT

Lord, many times I've prayed to thee
For you to open up a door
To help me with spiritual things
And for blessings to be poured

I feel I have a need at times
Impatiently waiting for the sign
And nothing seems to come my way
Pacing, watching everyday

You said to ask and you shall give
Seek and ye shall find
Knock and the door shall be opened for you
I can't find it perhaps it's disguised
Or am I a little blind

LORD I BELIEVE

I believe you can move mountains
I believe you do impossible things
I believe you're God Almighty
Omnipotent and supreme

I believe you still work miracles
Great big and little small
But Lord, I'm waiting patiently
I need more faith that's all

I believe you heal the sick
You alone raise the dead
I believe you give the Word of God
When your children need to be fed

I believe you forgive us when we ask
And you cleanse our hearts from sin
My petition to you Father
I need more faith within

I believe that faith is on its way
Forgive me when I doubt
I'll sit and wait for each new day
Let me rejoice and not pout

I believe you Jesus, I believe you Lord
For faith that you've restored
I thank you Jesus and thank you Lord
For I already have faith and more

NO REPUTION

He made himself of no reputation

He didn't boast of things he could do

He humbled himself and became lowly

Did you know He did it for you?

Did you know it was humiliating?

Yes, they laughed and called him names

They wouldn't accept Jesus as the Son of God

He was poor, uneducated, and didn't have any fame

PRAISE AND THANKSGIVING

Father, we give praise and thanks to you
For setting our spirits free
For the gift of my salvation
That was purchased on Calvary

Thank you for your love
And grace you freely give
Thank you for your Holy Word
That teaches us how to live

Thank you for the Holy Spirit
A teacher and comforter from thee
Strengthen and sustains us
You give power and Victory

REST AND WAIT

Rest in the Lord
And He will lead the way
Rest in the Lord my child
He'll never let you stray

When in the darkest hour
Afraid and you can't see
Believe and trust in Jesus
He promises to keep thee

Wait on the Lord
His main concern is you
Wait on the Lord my child
Why worry about what you should do

He'll meet your every need
No matter what it is
Remember He's your Father
And you're a child of his

SLIPPING AWAY

My life is not what I would like it to be

It seems as though I am slipping away from thee

The road I am traveling down

Seems so ragged and rough

I've got to travel it alone

But with Jesus I'll be strong, I'll be tough

People constantly telling me,

You're lost, that's not the right way

But I have news for you

Jesus is in control here today

No more pleasing men,

And their selfish foolish ways

For I'm striving to go home with Jesus

One of these ole days...

TIME ALONE WITH GOD

I love to have some time alone
And spend it Lord with thee
My quiet little talk with you
Brings peace and harmony

I love to give you my best chair
For you to watch me as I pray
And read the Word you've given me
Lord I get strength for the day

Lord I love to have some time alone
To give praise and give thanks to you
And humbly bow before thy throne
So I can glorify you too.

TRACES

Traces of the Lord, I can see
Throughout my whole life
He's watched over me
Never did he leave me all alone
But inside my heart
He made His home

Times did come
Suffering and sorrow were very real
But Jesus did comfort me
His grace lingers still
Traces of the Lord I can see
You know He still cares
And watches over me

WHO IS IT

Who is it that I may call?
Come work for me today
Who will be my servant?
Who will do just as I say?
Who is it who will follow?
Though the way you do not know
Who is it who will trust me?
When I say child, thou must go
Who is it, it is you child?
I've prepared you for this day
Obey my voice and trust in me
Your faith will lead the way

WORD OF GOD

We accept the Bible as God's written word

And preach salvation's message to those who've never

heard

We read it, and quote it, and try to live it to some

degree

Until arising situations that are not befitting unto thee

We begin to rationalize it, and say He didn't mean it so

They were written for the people a long, long time ago

You must take it as it is, do not add or take away

For the Word of God is holy and is written for us today

"For whatsoever things were written aforetime were
written for our learning that we through patience and
comfort of the scriptures might have hope" Romans
15:4

YOU WERE THERE

You were there during the hard times
When I was being abused
You were the only one who accepted me
When I was totally confused

You spent time, you listened
You wiped away my tears
You tried to raise my self-esteem
And chase away all my fears

You held me in the highest regard
When I could not see my worth
You told me I was special
When I wanted to curse my birth

You cherished, you loved
You patiently waited, you cared
You were always there for me
And willingly you shared

You said that I would make it
To hold up my head with pride
That you would always be faithful
You promised love and peace to abide inside…

Psalms of Life
love/marriage

AFRAID

I was afraid to give my love
To someone once again
For my little heart was bruised and scarred
And would take time to mend

But then I sought the Lord
To hear what He had to say
I am going to renew your love my child
But in return you give it away

I don't want this thing called love Lord
Too much pain and grief to bear
For people take and take and take and take
For who has the time to care

But child my love will begin to grow in you
And your eyes will be open to see
Wisdom, understanding, beauty and grace
And more do I have for thee
For it is only in giving love away
That you can freely receive

BECAUSE HE FIRST LOVED ME

Because He first loved me

God sent His son

Because He first loved me

To redeem the lost one

What love, what love

God has for me

Because He first loved me

Because He first loved me

God suffers long

Because He first loved me

His grace has not gone

What love what love

God has for me

Because He first loved me

Because He first loved me

God keeps me in His care

Because He first loved me

Yet willingly God has shared

His precious love with me

So I could give it unconditionally

Because He first loved me

EXPECTATIONS

I cannot expect you to do things
Because that's the way that I would
Nor can I expect it
Because I know that you should
I cannot change you
to make you think just like me
But I have to learn to love you
Unconditionally

I must love
Whether I get anything in return
To learn the precious lesson
That love cannot be earned
If you give it, and give it
Totally unconditionally
Jesus will return it to you
One day, unexpectedly

FILLED WITH YOUR LOVE

Oh to be filled with your love
So all the world can see
More and more of Jesus
And less and less of me

Oh to be filled with perfect love
My total heart body soul and mind
Completely surrendered to the Father's will
Showering love to all mankind

Oh to be filled with your love, Lord
Is my prayer I offer to you
That the Son will be glorified in my little life
In the things I say and do

GOD'S LOVE

Jesus loves me this I know

For through the pages of the Bible

It clearly tells me so

But just how much does Jesus love me

I cannot understand

For His love cannot be measured

By any instrument of man

I know He loved me very much

To come and die for me

And he asked His Father to forgive me

When He hung on Calvary

I know He loves me very much

For He cleanses me from sin and shame

And He really knows me personally

For He calls me by my name

There is nothing that can separate

God's precious love from me

Not height, nor depth, nor life, or death

Not even angles or principalities

For none of these are able

To separate God's love from me

For Jesus' love is enduring

Oh people can't you see

Nor things past, present, or things to come

You can say that my God's love is

Special, Genuine, and number one

JESUS

So patiently you've waited and waited and waited
Without stretched arms for me
Thinking of all the pain, heartache, sorrow
You suffered on Calvary

With a perfect love, you have loved us
Though so sinful was all mankind
So forgiving, yet so humble and meek
Lord, you never even seemed to mind

You took off your crown, you laid down your life
And you left all your power up there
Even though I didn't deserve it
You're the true and living God who cares

JESUS IS THE ONLY WAY

I have many tears that I do weep
But they are not tears of sorrow
That fills my cheeks

Oh! But the love, the joy,
The happiness I have found
The love of Jesus that truly abounds

It fills my heart within
The love of Jesus is always there
Oh! Today I challenge you to seek Him

Let Him lead and guide you each day
For you will truly find
That Jesus is the only way

JUST WANTED

I just wanted to love you
To show you a better way
How Jesus came into my life
How he brightened up my day

I just wanted to let you know
There is someone who really cares
Through the trials and tribulations
The Lord Jesus wants to share

I just wanted to let you know
The real peace you could have inside
By surrendering your will to Jesus
Let Him be your guide

I just wanted you to know
The Lord has paved the way
Open up the doors of your heart
And let Jesus come in today

PAIN HE SUFFERED

The pain that He had suffered
The burdens He carried there
While people laughed and spat on Him
Do you think they really cared?

Separated from His father
Jesus was praying for you and me
Heavenly Father, please, for them
Please lay this charge to me

He asked His Father to forgive us
Because He loved us so
He promised us eternal life
Salvation is free you know

PICTURE OF LOVE

I must paint the picture of love
To show you the price Jesus paid
For Jesus truly loved us
Salvation was what He gave

He said Father for give them
For they know not what they do
This is the prayer that Jesus prayed
When He hung on the cross for you

They nailed His hands and feet
To that old rugged cross
He humbly stayed upon it
So the world would not be lost

They mocked Him and they beat Him
And they pierced Him in His side
He asked His Father to forgive them
As His heart anguished inside

He suffered and He bled
Gave up His Spirit to His Father up above
He did it all for you and me
This was His sacrificial love

Judas was the one who betrayed Him
And He did it with a kiss
Pilate found no fault in Him
And His case he tried to dismiss

The people cried crucify Him
Do not let Him get away
For we want the release of Barrabas
Release him now this day

The disciples they all ran scared
For they didn't know what to do

They too betrayed our Savior and Lord
And that is just like me and you

SACRED MARRIAGE VOW

Father, consecrate this marriage
In the name of Jesus we pray
Teach us to love one another
To respect, to forgive, to obey

Teach us to follow your leading
Teach us to lean on you
Teach us to include you Father
In all we think, feel, say, or do

Teach us heavenly Father
The agape love from above
Knit our hearts together
And wrap it in this love

Teach us how to hold on
When the way gets hard to bear
Teach us to how to be patient
To endure, to encourage, and to care

Teach us how to give our all
And not just a little part
Let nothing come between us lord
Let not evil root in our hearts

Father consecrate this marriage
In the name of Jesus we pray
That we might glorify you
In our marriage each and every day
That the twain may be as one flesh O Lord
Let our marriage glorify you everyday

SHATTERED IN PART

It was only the Lord
Who brought me through
For I tried everything
That I could possibly do

When I was broken in pieces
And shattered in parts
Only then could Jesus
Fix my broken heart

I was helpless, mixed up
All scrambled around
This is when
His love I found

Little by little
He began to make me new
So now I can share
His love with you

SHUT OUT

There is no communication

Between you and me

I'll have to be honest

I feel you are pulling away

I want you to know

I'm praying for you everyday

I ask you for forgiveness

For whatever I've said or done

I have no intentions

Of hurting God's chosen one

I'm soliciting your prayers

Continuously pray for me

For as a child I am learning

And I always stand in need

THE COVENANT

This couple is gathered together
And has sought your approval from above
To be united in Holy Matrimony
And to be filled with Agape' love

They have made a commitment to each other
That no matter what they go through
They would seek your direction and guidance
And bond closer and closer to you

Knowing selfish desires will come
Where they must choose to lay down their lives
Where Agape' love continues to give in
And a freedom to serve you doth arise

So Father, have your way in this marriage
May we always bring glory and honor to you
As we give ourselves to each other
In the things we say and do

WELL LORD HERE AM I

Well Lord, here am I
Can't run anymore
And I am too tried to try
Don't know what to do
Don't know where to go
I can't fool you anymore
So I decided to take it slow

Well Lord, here am I
I'm sick of myself
So I'll let you try
Take me as I am
Do with me as you may
Cleanse my heart
And take my sins away

Put a right spirit
Deep within my heart
Lord, you promised me
A brand new start

Shower me with your love
Sprinkle it on me everyday
And let me share your love
With someone on my way

YOU ARE MY PARTNER FOR LIFE

You are my partner for life
And I want you to know that my love is true
There isn't anything that you might ask of me
That I as your wife would not do

God has given you the wisdom
And understanding in so many ways
To discern my thoughts and feelings
And to meet my needs each day

You are the spiritual leader
Yes, you protect and cover me
So I surrender my will to you
Just remember to love me continuously

ABOUT THE AUTHOR

Carolyn Stovall was born in Lincoln, Nebraska to Bettye (Lewis) and Calvin Rodgers. Carolyn has been married to retired SMSGT Ted Stovall since 1974 and they have two daughters, Brooke Awan and Sarah Alvarado. They also have five grandchildren who are their hearts joy, Noah, Caleb, Faith, Seth, Solomon.

She received her spiritual training at an early age through her grandmother Sarah Tarpley. Her life-long passion for community service is the result of the impact the church made on her early life.

Carolyn has a B.A. in Psychology and Sociology and a minor in Women Studies from Bellevue College (Bellevue, Nebraska). She also has a Masters in Community Counseling from St. Mary's University (San Antonio, Texas). Carolyn has worked and served in San Antonio as a Psychotherapist and has recently retired.

Carolyn Stovall has volunteered in churches and communities everywhere her family was stationed. She currently volunteers at BAMSI military hospital. Regarding her work, Carolyn says, "There are so many people with special needs, so many tasks, and too few people to do them. I feel I have been blessed, so to sacrifice my time and talent is the least I can do to spread Christ's love to a hurting world."

Carolyn is a member of Lackland Air Force Base Permanent Party Chapel and attends its Gospel Service, where she has taught Bible studies for over 20 years and is a member of the Gospel Choir. She has also been a guest speaker at many churches and Women's Retreats around the country where she has also shared her gift of poetry.

Made in the USA
Monee, IL
02 March 2020